Collection of Concious

Cait Power

Presentation by *BookLeaf Publishing*

Web: www.bookleafpub.com

E-mail: info@bookleafpub.com

ISBN: 978-93-95755-66-5

First edition 2022

To Mister, Pickle, Baby Squid and Bubbie

Without you I am nothing

You

Dandelion seeds
Dancing at the pathways end
Beautiful like you

How it is

All your intentions can fall
like sand through your fingers
Feathers on the wind
You can follow the instructions but still be
unable to bring it to fruition
A missing puzzle piece
A smile can be misinterpreted by the view of
those behind the eyes
Fleeting flirt
Stupid scorn
There will be times
where nothing will go to plan
However how much you prepare
A wilted flower on the verge of bloom

And sometimes, that's just how it is.

The Bond

The blossoms were pink
Soft like satin and full of honey bees
They stood on tall branches
Taller than the men's heads
The men smiled
Behind eyes
Crinkled with age
They shared a laugh
As old as they
From the time they were boys
The bond between brothers
Never fades I see
Still just two little boys
Giggling together
About the frog they hid
In their sister's shoe

Why

Why tell me they think I'm fat and ugly
When I needed to hear I was beautiful
Why tell me I didn't have the patience
When I just needed hope
Why treat my illness like a personal attack
When I just need help
Why make me the reason for your bad mood
When you could have just been honest
Why blame me for things going wrong
When I had suggestions to fix them
Why treat me like a whore
When you know I was always home
Why teach me that the world is full of liars and
cheats
When it was always you
Why act like it's just a joke
When no one else is laughing
Why hold everything else in higher esteem
When I thought only of you
Why dictate my actions
When your life is shambles

Why did you become a mother
When you couldn't even love yourself

Mama

It's 5 o'clock in the morning
A damp misty morning
Totally silent
Except for the steady drumming of rain
Suddenly a small black squirrel
Dashes from her nest in the shed
To the relative shelter of the cedar bush
She has stored some acorns
In the dead ash tree
Her barking increases
As she dashed around the tree
Pulling free chunks of dead bark
In her desperate search
For the food she saved
Other small faces appear
At the hole in the shed
What will she do with no acorns
Her family is hungry
So she sets off into the rain once more

Old Soul Lifesaver

You came into my life
A lifesaver in the ocean
Saving me from drowning
In my own stupidity
And loss of control.
You were wise
An old soul they called you
My beautiful baby.
We spent all our time together
Bobbing along in the ocean
Of my own creation.
Floating past islands and harbors
That could offer us shelter.
A new way of life.
But I was blinded by the sun on the water
Didn't see that to hold me afloat
You must always be half drowned.
We continue through the waves
And I try to hold you beside me instead.
I need to let go I realize
So you can float away.
I know then where I went wrong
And I wish I had stopped to build us a boat.

Brainstipation

Blocked
In over my head
But I have so many words
Inside my head
Ready to tell a story
But I feel like a fraud
Are my words too cultivated
Too raw
I can't describe the sunset
the senses overwhelm
And again I feel
Blocked

To Us

I feel so much gratitude to you
For who you are
And for who I am when I'm with you
We raised our children together
And they are turning out amazing
Just like you
Just like us
That night I got sick
And you hugged me
While I cried
On the side on the highway
In Toronto of all places
It hasn't always been easy
But at every turn you're there
To support and encourage me
Every stumbling block
We overcome together
Cements my commitment to you
And we use those bricks
To build a home
For us

Petrol

My love is a flaming watering can
Filled with petrol and set ablaze
Dutifully I water my plants
What should be nurturing water
Is slowly tuning them to ash
They cannot see the flames
And can't understand
Why I am now smothering them

Open Season

Happy smiling faces
Or feet and bags dragging on the ground
There can be no getting around
The return to school
Though I pray
That stays the case
I know it's a cliché
But that doesn't make it less true
No parent should have to burry their baby
And I can't understand how
These things can keep happening
How we refuse to learn from it
And make real changes
For real change
Hell if I was america
I could use my spare change
And change a whole families trajectory
Forever

It hurts

Everything hurts
It's inside my skin
Inside my head
And I can't let it win
My soul feels its weight
It's only the world
The pain and sadness
New life unfurled
The rage and destruction
My shoulders can hold it
But how can it change
When they don't care one bit

Summer Night

The only sound is the cicadas
There's a soft cool breeze
My heart feels slow
And calm
A humming bird appears
Hovering perfectly still
Then flitting away
As the day wears on
The sunlight is filtering
Through the needles and leaves
The way it shimmers
It feels completely magical
A bevvey of woodland creatures
Join us for tea
And as the sun sets
The sky fills with bats
Crickets have replaced
The calls of cicada
The sky is filled with stars

I am

The breeze on the wind
Carry me out to the sea
I hate who I was
But I love who is me
I am creative and caring
So loving, opinionated
My own code of conduct
From outside seems outdated
But I hated growing up
Feeling more like old stuff
And if I dared say so
You'd leave in a huff
So I turned to self harm
As a means of attaining
The showoff my friends got
From your First-aid training
Nothing ever works out like we plan
I only make you mad
I ruined the bed and all your plans
Of the rainbow baby you wish you'd had
It shaped the way I thought
Spoke about myself and cared
I assumed the world was mean and cruel
I always felt alone and scared
Now I'm much better

Had to relearn everything
But I love who I am
Kind, hopeful, interesting

Wednesday

15

Pulling yourself up by your bootstraps
Was meant to be impossible
Not the standard of how we cope
Mother Thereasa hated her job
Yet we idolize her actions
And brand her a Saint
We expect the poor to give their all
While emptying our water bottles
Onto the dirt because it's warm now
No concept of what others go through
Ye we believe our thoughts and prayers can heal
But antidepressants can't cure poverty

Pets

Some days I realize that this is likely your last
summer with us
So I make sure to spend as much time out in the
sun with you as I can
Sometimes I feel sad because I know I could
have done better
I also know that I was your whole world and in
your eyes did no wrong
We honestly don't deserve the love and devotion
Our animal companions give to us
But I am eternally grateful to each animal who
has blessed my life
So I will spend more days in the grass with you
Longer walks many more cuddles
You might be here short time for me
However we will have so much fun
Because for you this is everything

Anxiety

I feel paralyzed
Like I'm shaking violently
Yet it's all inside
There's a roaring
In my head constantly
Like I'm inside a waterfall
It's impossible to think
To form a sentence
Too many things happening at once
Sometimes I think I could just scream
All the anxiety out of me
Like a powerful roar
The only sound I muster
Is a tired wheezing sigh

Birds

18

Watching you soar through the sky
Dipping together in a cloud
A murmuration of birds
Such variety of size, shape, and colour
Were I a bird
I would join your flock
The thrill of flight
Just the thought of it
Makes my heart race

Lieku

19

I put too much faith
In the lie that was your love
So conditional

Narcissus

20

I feel so sorry
For your beautiful children
They deserved better

Ending

It seems I've wasted
A lot of time
Other people's and my own
And my thoughts
Come out like globs
I can't think unless I'm alone
I cry a lot
Like way too much
My eyes get puffed and raw
And other people
Have it worse you know
Yes I know I saw
Don't forget
Other people's journeys
Really are their own
They way we cope
From thing to thing
Is unique to you alone
So try to help
Whenever you can
You never know who needs it
And extra love
To you the reader
Your support means quite a bit